FORTNITE

THIS BOOK BELONGS TO

____

____

TEST COLOR PAGE

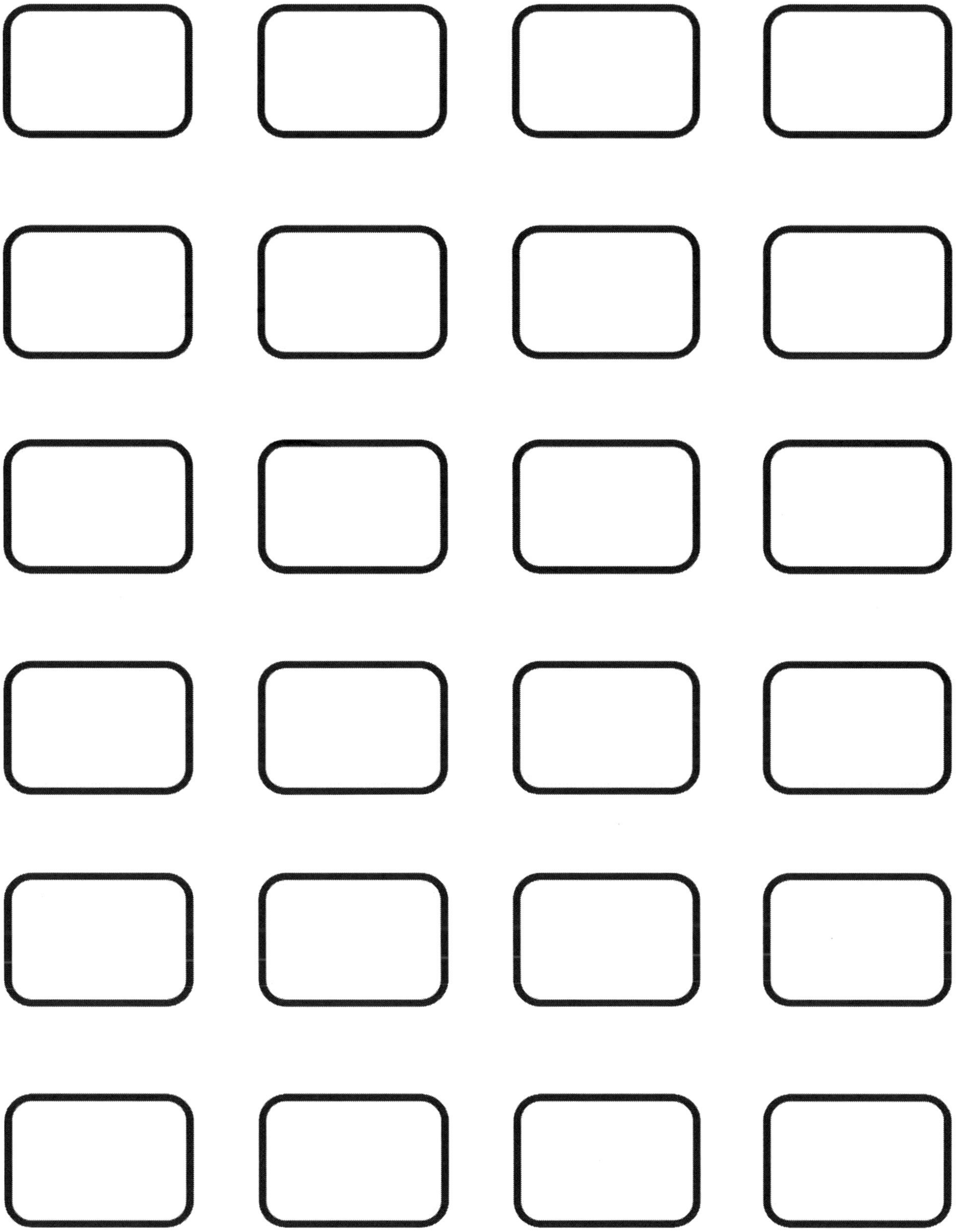

FORTNITE
BATTLE
ROYALE

FORTNITE
BATTLE
ROYALE

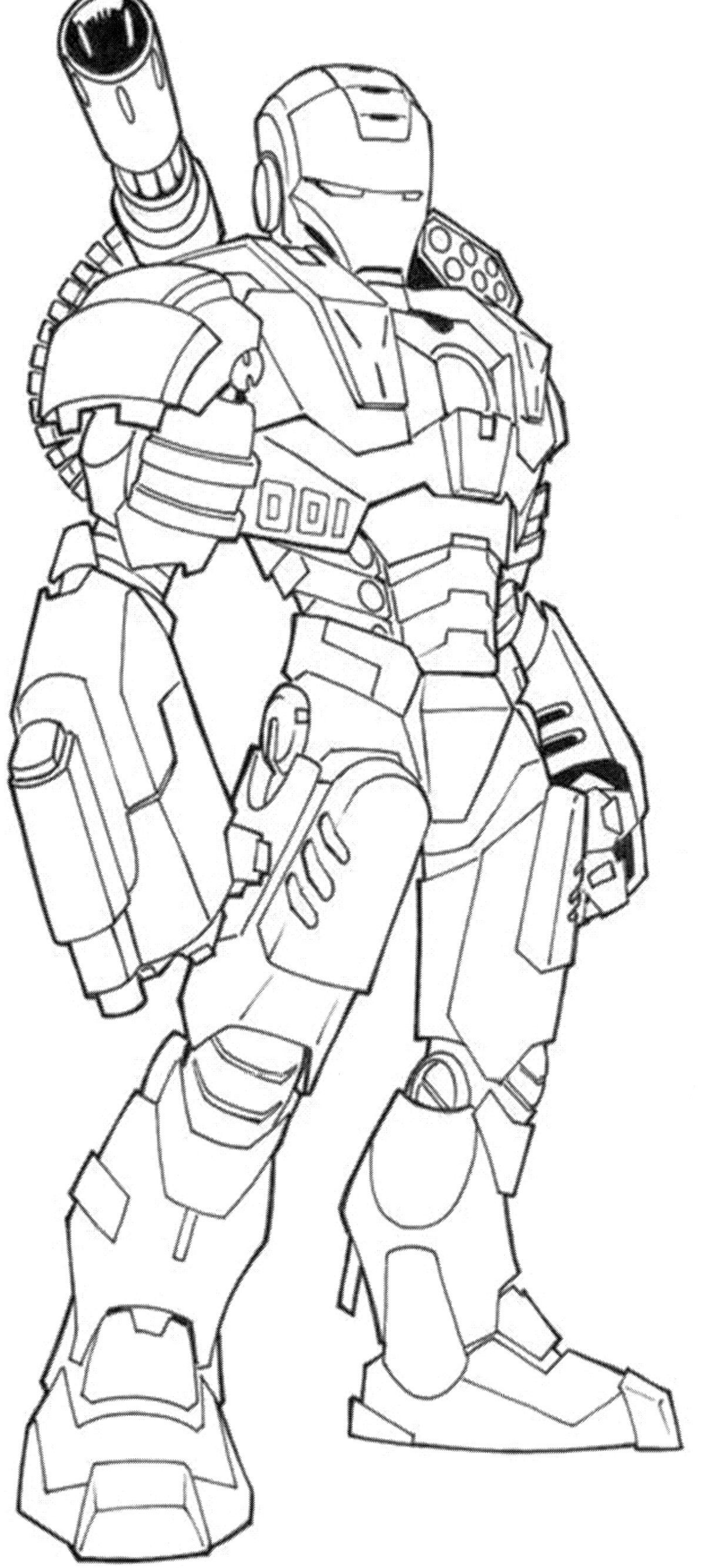

FORTNITE
BATTLE
ROYALE

FORTNITE
BATTLE
ROYALE

Brite Bomber

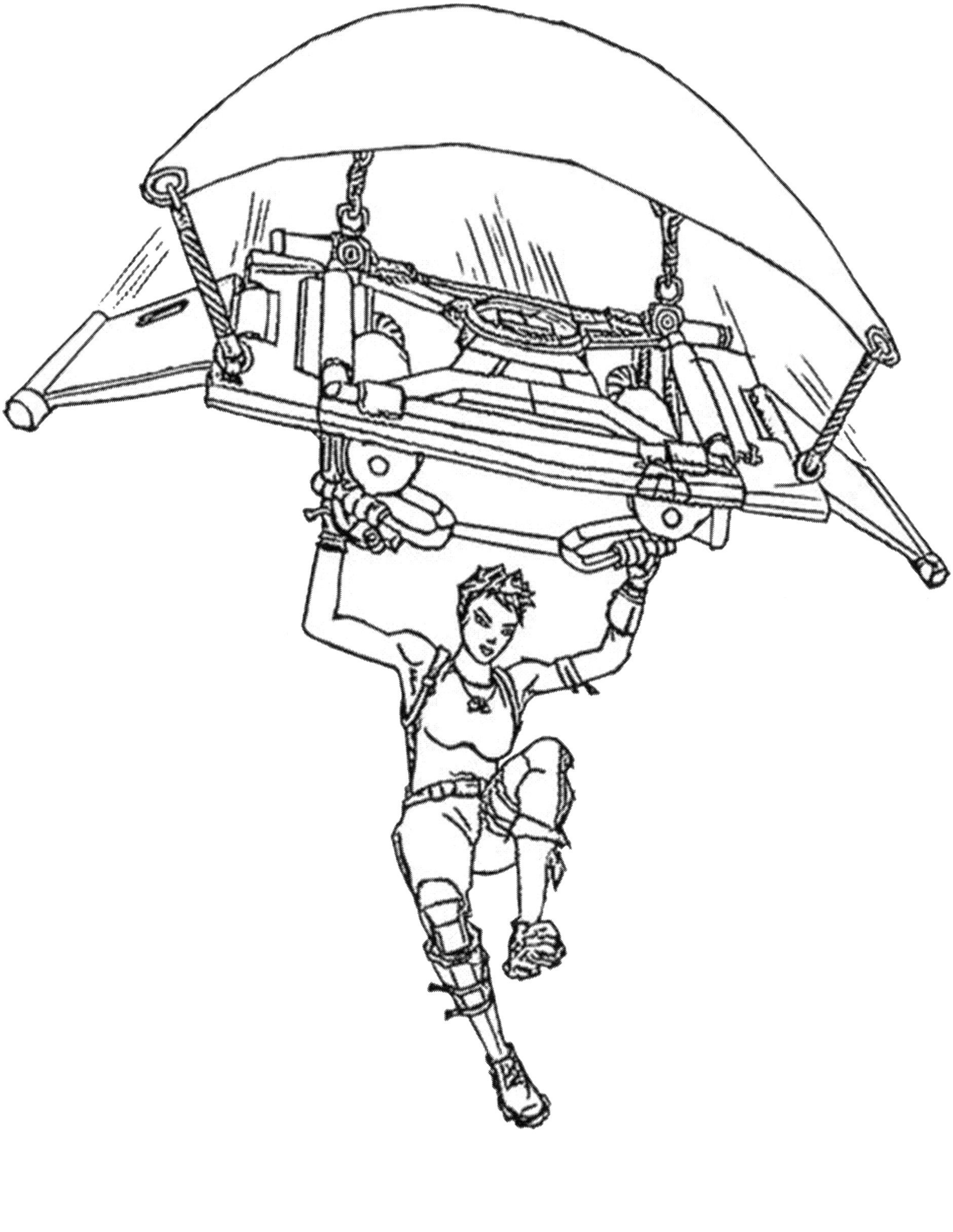

FORTNITE
BATTLE
ROYALE

FORTNITE
SEASON 9

DEADPOOL

FORTNITE

FORTNITE
SEASON 7

FORTNITE
SEASON 9

Omega

FORTNITE
SEASON 8

FORTNITE
BATTLE
ROYALE

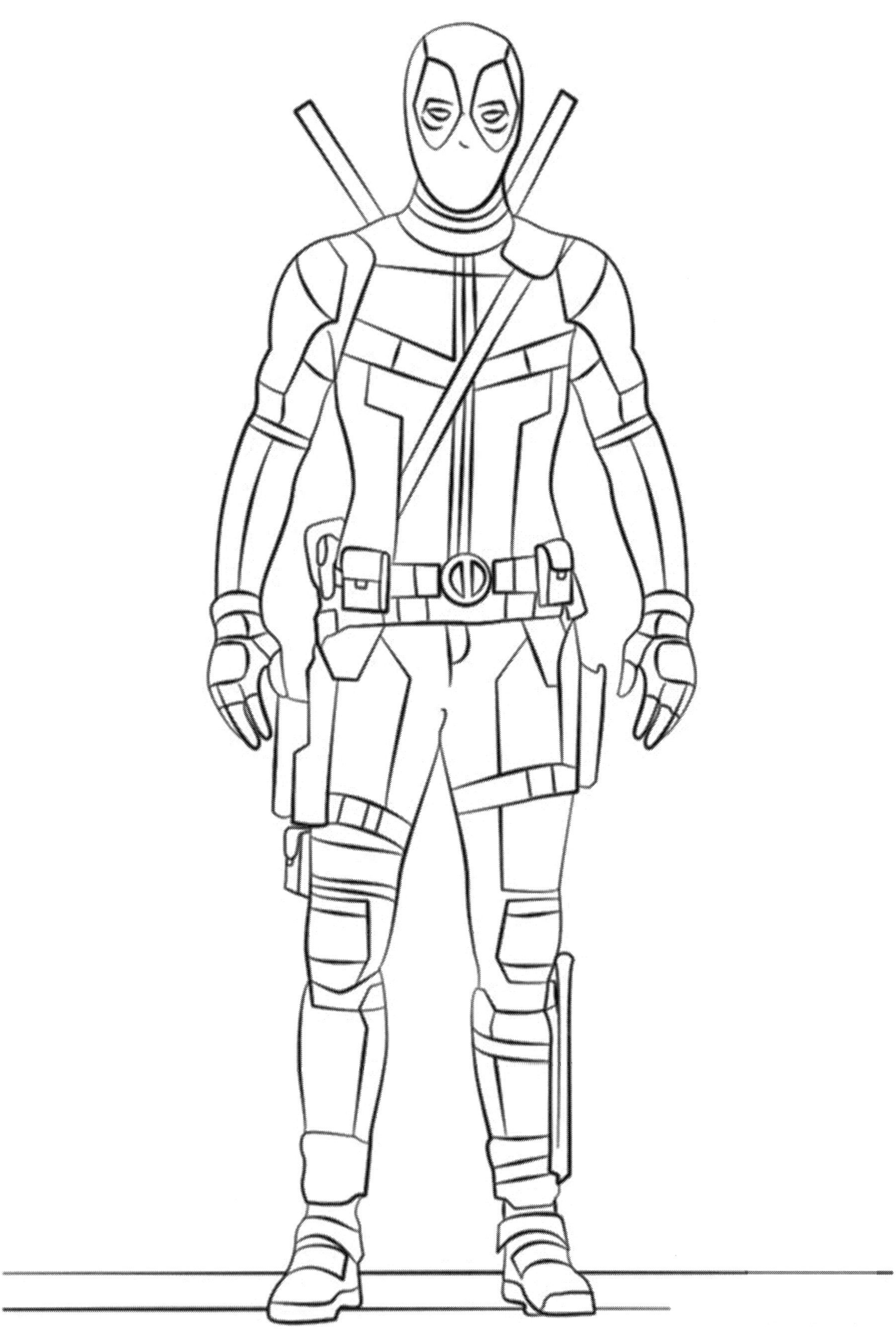

FORTNITE
SEASON 9

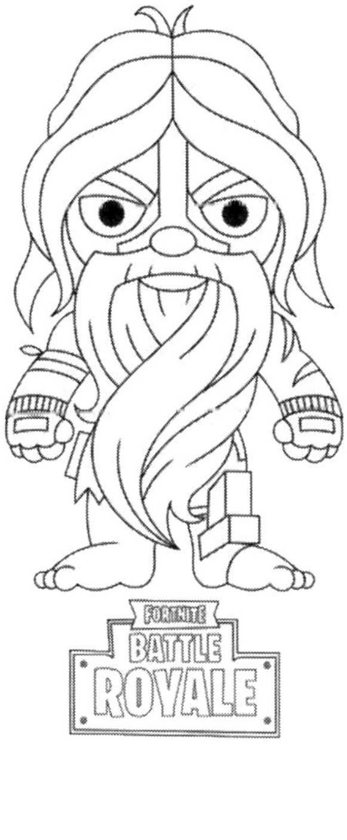

FORTNITE
BATTLE
ROYALE

FORTNITE
BATTLE
ROYALE

FORTNITE
BATTLE
ROYALE

Rook

FORTNITE
SEASON 8

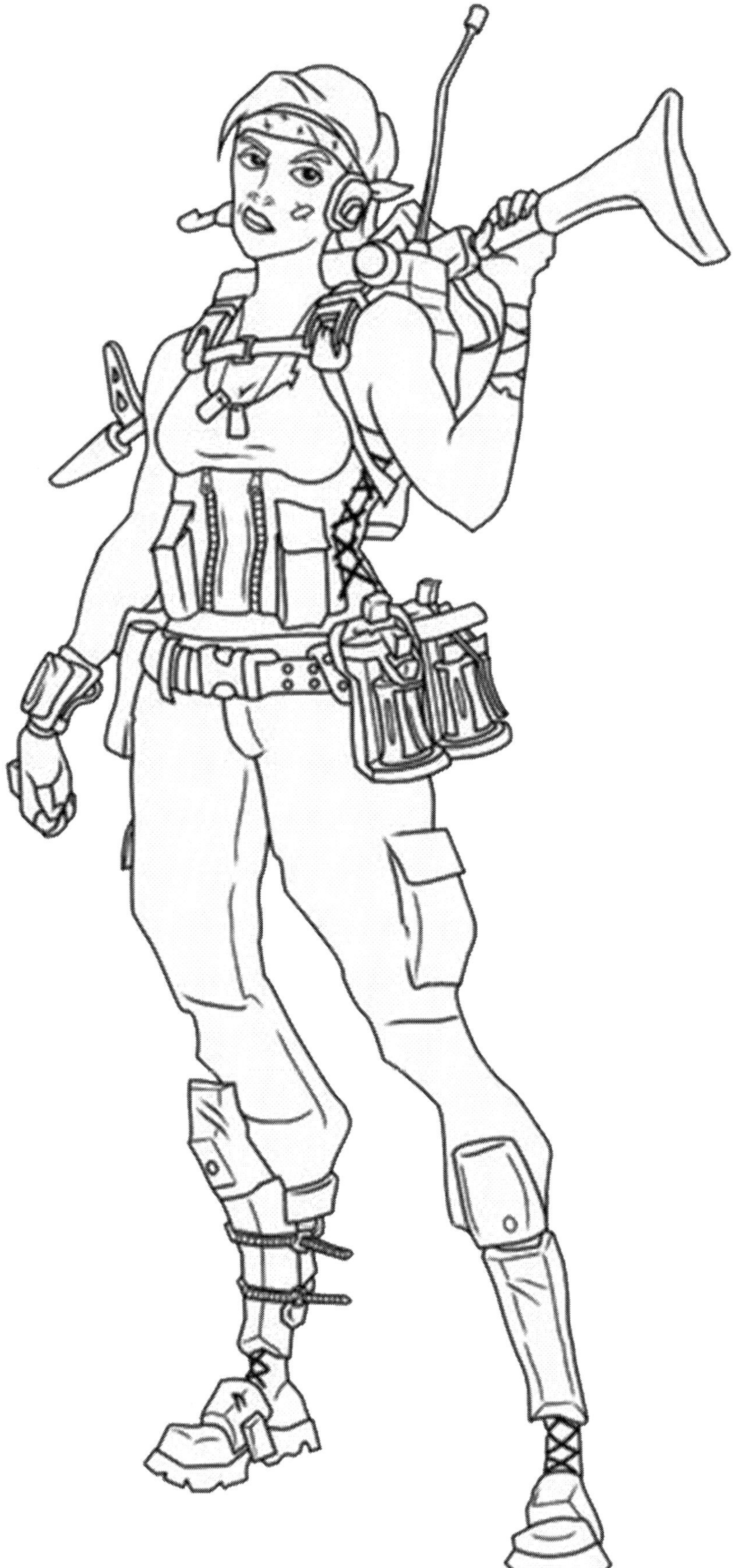

FORTNITE
BATTLE
ROYALE

FORTNITE
BATTLE
ROYALE

FORTNITE
SEASON 7

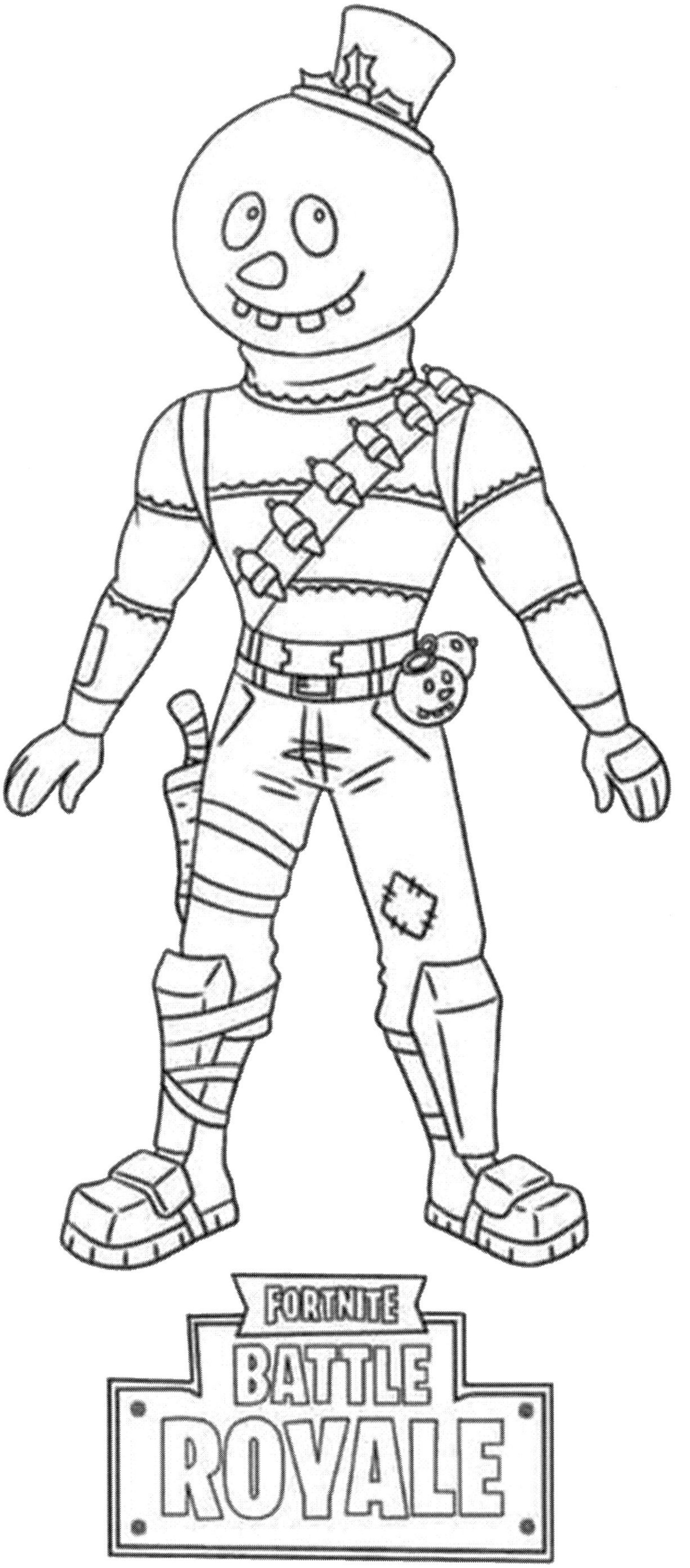

FORTNITE
BATTLE
ROYALE

FORTNITE
BATTLE
ROYALE

FORTNITE
SEASON 8

IKONIK

FORTNITE
SEASON 9

FORTNITE
BATTLE
ROYALE

FORTNITE
SEASON 7

FORTNITE
BATTLE
ROYALE

FORTNITE

FORTNITE
BATTLE
ROYALE

FORTNITE
SEASON 10

FORTNITE BATTLE ROYALE

Zoey

Manufactured by Amazon.ca
Bolton, ON

15334235R00057